THE
EASTER
ACTIVITY
BOOK

Illustrated by Dan Hayes

Ideals Children's Books • Nashville, Tennessee

ISBN 0-8249-8499-4

The Story of Easter

Easter is probably the most important holiday in Christianity. And while we celebrate the rebirth of spring at this time, it is Jesus' Resurrection which is the true reason for the celebration of Easter.

Jesus had been healing and teaching the people about God, gathering followers everywhere he went. When the time came for him to fulfill the prophecies which foretold his death and Resurrection, Jesus journeyed to Jerusalem for the traditional Passover celebration. The people greeted him as a king, lining the streets and covering the ground with their cloaks and palm fronds. This was the first Palm Sunday.

Jesus made his way to the temple in Jerusalem to pray and to teach, but instead he found that money changers and merchants had set up booths there. He became angry and knocked down the booths. He drove the merchants away, then went into the temple to pray.

As more and more people gathered about to hear Jesus preach, the leaders of the temple became fearful of him. They began plotting to have him arrested.

Four nights later, Jesus and his twelve disciples gathered together for the traditional Passover meal. Jesus held a loaf of bread and gave thanks to God. He broke the loaf into pieces and gave it to his disciples. Then he passed around his cup so that each disciple could drink from it.

After supper, Jesus and several of his disciples went to the Garden of Gethsemane. Jesus left his friends and went among the trees to pray. Each time he returned to his disciples, he found them sleeping. As he tried to awaken them on his third return, a group of Roman soldiers arrived, accompanied by temple officials. They arrested Jesus and took him to the high priests.

When Jesus would not deny that he was the Son of God, the high priests turned him over to the Roman ruler, Pontius Pilate.

Pilate could not find fault with Jesus, but the chief priests had stirred up the crowd. Afraid to make a decision, Pilate asked the crowd if he should release Jesus. But the crowd cried out, "Crucify him!" So Jesus was taken away by the soldiers, crowned with thorns, and crucified.

At the moment of his death, the sky became dark, a great earthquake shook the earth, and the great curtain in the temple was ripped in half from top to bottom.

Jesus' body was taken down from the cross by one of his followers and gently laid in a tomb. A huge stone was rolled in front of the tomb and a soldier was sent to stand guard.

Early Sunday morning, the third day after Christ's death, a group of women arrived at the tomb to anoint his body. They cried out when they discovered that his body was gone. An angel appeared and told the women that Christ had risen. Soon his disciples and family and friends had learned of Jesus' Resurrection.

And when Jesus appeared to his friends again, he told them to go throughout the world, telling all the people what they had seen and heard. And he made a promise to them: "Wherever you go, I will be there with you always, even until the end of time."

And thus is the promise of Easter—we rejoice because Jesus died for us and was risen. And we know that because he lives, we, too, can live.

Decorating Easter Eggs

Ingredients:

eggs, 1 to 2 dozen
white vinegar
food coloring

Equipment:

1 large saucepan
timer
1 small saucepan

8 oz. ceramic or glass cups, 1 for each color
table spoon
teaspoon
paper towels

1. Gently place eggs in saucepan and cover with cold tap water.

2. Place saucepan on stove and turn burner on medium high.

3. When eggs begin to boil, set a timer for 10 minutes.

4. After timer goes off, remove saucepan from stove and pour out hot water. Cover eggs with cold water and let stand.

5. Fill small saucepan with half cup of water for each dye. Place on stove with burner set on high, and let come to a boil. Remove from heat.

6. Fill each cup halfway with boiling water.

7. Add 1 teaspoon white vinegar to each cup.

8. Stir 15 to 25 drops food color into each cup. Most food color packages contain red, blue, green, and yellow. If you would like purple, add 15 drops red and 5 drops blue. For orange, use 15 drops yellow and 5 drops red.

9. Using table spoon, place one egg in each cup. For pastel colors, leave egg in cup for only a moment or two. The longer the egg stands in the color, the darker the shade will be.

10. Place wet eggs on paper towels to dry.

NOTE: Use these directions for creating dyes for all of the decorating ideas on the following pages.

Two-toned Eggs

1. Dip entire egg into first color of choice. Leave in only a short time, so that base color is light. Allow egg to dry completely.

2. Dip egg into second color of choice only as far as you want color to extend.

3. Dry egg on paper towel with freshly dipped side down so that color does not run.

Striped Eggs

1. Dye egg a base color or leave white.

2. Place snug-fitting rubber bands around egg. Use wide or narrow bands, depending on the width of stripes that you want.

3. Dip egg into desired color. Remove and allow to dry completely.

4. Once color has dried, remove rubber bands to expose your stripes.

Tie-dyed Eggs

1. Wrap eggs in a small piece of lightweight cloth.

2. Twist tightly and secure each end with a tie or rubber band.

3. Dip egg into desired color. Allow egg to sit until cloth is completely dry.

4. Remove cloth to reveal your design.

Marbled Eggs

1. Wrap egg in a damp piece of lightweight cloth.

2. Lightly twist and secure each end.

3. Drop spots of color onto the cloth. Repeat with additional colors, if desired.

4. Twist the cloth more tightly around the egg so that the colors will blend together.

5. Unwrap egg to reveal your pattern.

Personalized Eggs

1. Using a white crayon or a small wax stick, write your name or the name of a family member or friend on your egg.

2. Dip the egg into the desired color. The wax will resist the dye, leaving the name in white while the rest of the egg is colored.

Decorator Eggs

1. Dye egg to desired color or leave white, if preferred.

2. Gather an arrangement of decorations, such as yarn, ribbon, buttons, sequins, and glitter.

3. Use liquid glue to draw a design on your egg. Sprinkle glitter over glue or apply ribbon or yarn to glue design.

4. Paste on buttons or sequins or other ornaments, as desired.

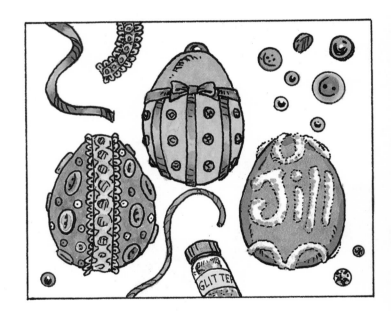

Painted Eggs

1. Dye egg to desired color or leave white, if preferred.

2. Use fabric paint to make patterns or designs on egg.

3. Paint egg one side at a time, allowing to dry between painting.

NOTE: Check to be sure paint has not bled through shell before eating. Discard egg if there is any sign of bleed-through on egg.

Comic Strip Eggs

1. Dye egg to desired color or leave white, if preferred.

2. Cut out characters from your favorite cartoon strip or comic book. Apply to egg with liquid glue or art paste.

NOTE: You can apply just one character or create a scene with additional characters and cut-out words for dialogue.

Egg Characters

1. Dye egg to desired color or leave white, if preferred.

2. Using crayons, paints, or markers, draw facial features on your egg.

3. Use construction paper, cotton balls, and buttons to make faces hair, ears, wings, tails, or whatever other parts your characters may need.

NOTE: Check egg before eating for any sign of bleed-through from markers or paints. Discard egg if any is present.

Egg Stands

To create a stand for your egg, simply cut a 1-inch strip of construction paper that is long enough to wrap around the base of your egg, allowing about a half inch for overlap. Decorate your stand as desired, then glue ends together. Let dry. Now put your egg in your stand.

Weave an Easter Basket

This beautiful basket is for decoration. It is too delicate to use for carrying anything heavy. It makes a candy dish, or, filled with potpourri, it is a nice Easter gift for someone you love. Younger children will need an adult's assistance with this project.

Materials:

construction paper (12" x 18")	scissors
pencil	glue
ruler	paper clips

1. Measure, draw, and cut 1-inch wide, vertical strips of paper. (You can use any color you like, or a combination of colors.)

2. Cut 4 inches off six of the strips so that they measure 14 inches each. These are your basket strips.

3. Fold basket strips into thirds and arrange them so that their center thirds form the circular bottom of the basket while their end thirds fold up.

4. Glue the basket strips together and let dry.

5. Use four 18-inch strips for weaving. Starting at the bottom of the basket, glue one end of a weaving strip to the inside of a basket strip. Paper clip the glued spot so that it will not come apart while you weave.

6. Bring the weaving strip outside of the next basket strip, then take in inside the next basket strip, and so on until it meets its other end. Trim off excess paper and glue the ends of the weaving strip together inside the basket. Let dry.

7. Remove the paper clip. Start your next weaving strip on the inside of another basket strip, and follow direction number 6. Make sure that you are following the opposite inside-outside weaving pattern from your first weaving strip. Use this same method for weaving your third and fourth strips.

8. Apply a stripe of glue to the back of an 18-inch strip and wrap this strip around the top of your basket. Trim off excess paper if desired, and paper clip to hold this strip on while it dries.

9. Trim the last strip to measure 15 inches. Glue each end to the inside of the basket to form a handle. Let your basket dry completely before using.

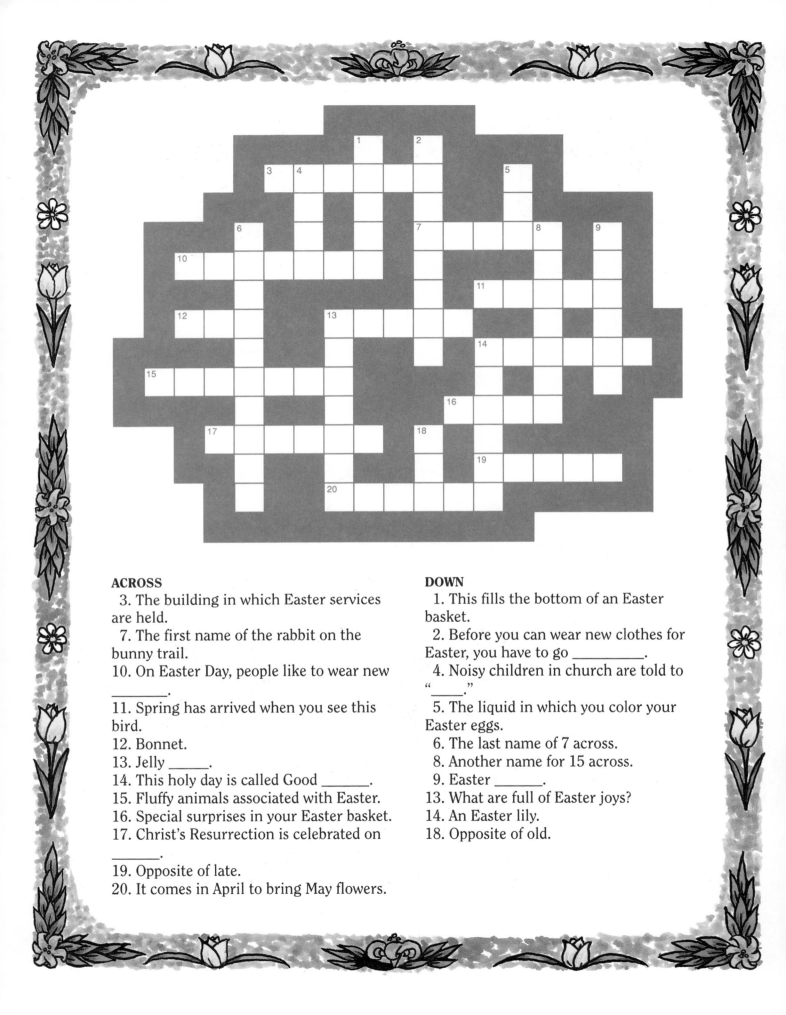

ACROSS

3. The building in which Easter services are held.
7. The first name of the rabbit on the bunny trail.
10. On Easter Day, people like to wear new _____.
11. Spring has arrived when you see this bird.
12. Bonnet.
13. Jelly _____.
14. This holy day is called Good _____.
15. Fluffy animals associated with Easter.
16. Special surprises in your Easter basket.
17. Christ's Resurrection is celebrated on _____.
19. Opposite of late.
20. It comes in April to bring May flowers.

DOWN

1. This fills the bottom of an Easter basket.
2. Before you can wear new clothes for Easter, you have to go _____.
4. Noisy children in church are told to "____."
5. The liquid in which you color your Easter eggs.
6. The last name of 7 across.
8. Another name for 15 across.
9. Easter _____.
13. What are full of Easter joys?
14. An Easter lily.
18. Opposite of old.

Humpty Dumpty Connect-the-Dots

Humpty Dumpty sat on a wall.
Humpty Dumpty had a great fall.
All the King's horses
And all the King's men
Couldn't put Humpty together again.
MOTHER GOOSE

Can you put Humpty together again in this Easter connect-the-dots game? Start with number 1 and draw a line connecting each number to the one which comes next. Once you've put Humpty back together, you can color him with bright Easter colors!

An Old-Fashioned Easter

Assembly instructions
are on following page.

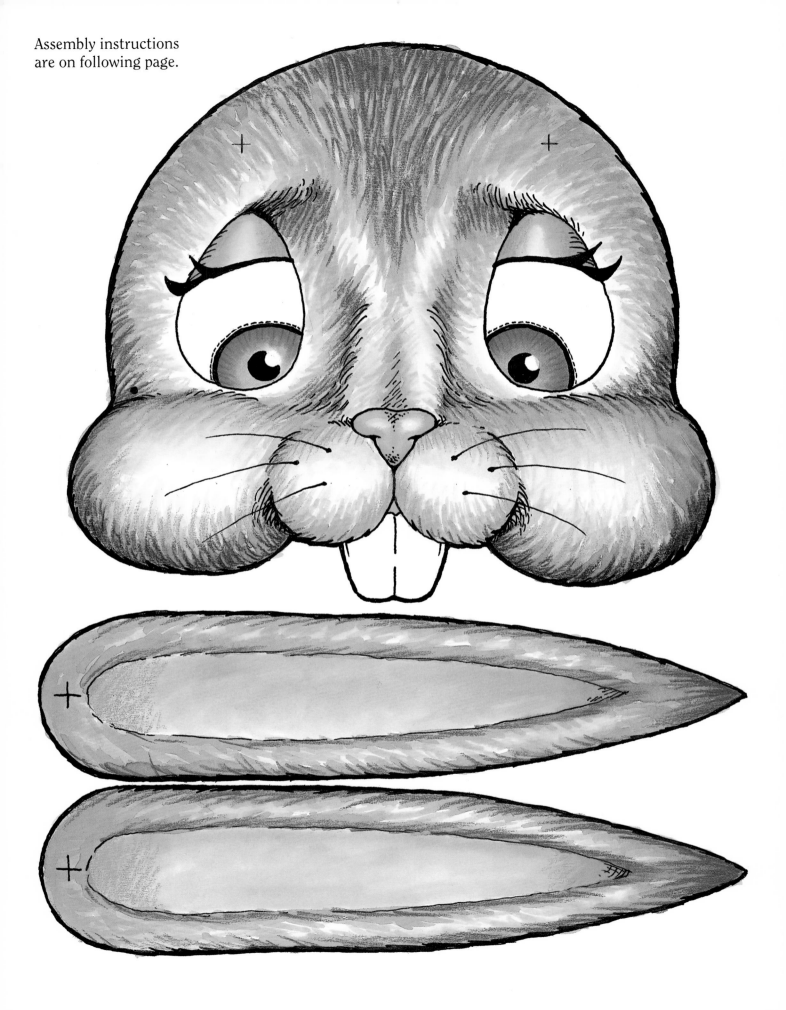